100 DAYS OF SUMMER READING

Book One:
100 Book Challenge

Leigh Lowe

MEMORIA PRESS
www.MemoriaPress.com

ISBN 978-1-61538-883-7

First Edition

INTRODUCTION

Traditionally, there are approximately 100 days of summer from Memorial Day to Labor Day. The **100 Books in 100 Days Challenge** asks students to read one book each day during the summer break from school (of course, you could pick any 100 days). Certainly this is a lofty goal! Accepting this challenge, however, affords many rewards.

1. **PRACTICE**: It is important for students who are just learning to read fluidly to maintain momentum and consistency. As we know, practice is important to the development of any new skill. Reading is no exception. 100 days is a lot of time in which new reading skills can be developed and improved upon—or forgotten! Let's choose practice!
2. **DISCIPLINE**: Rather than seeing reading as a chore or merely an assignment, we want students to recognize reading as a pleasure of great worth! Achieving this perspective often requires overcoming initial reluctance. The **100 Books in 100 Days Challenge** helps establish reading as an expectation, a habit, and ultimately a joy! Small comforts and routines can do much to promote the discipline of reading daily—a favorite chair, a special snack, a regular time of day. Find ways to make the daily habit of reading enjoyable.
3. **DISCERNMENT**: Encouraging and enabling students to recognize quality literature is a prime goal. As such, training in discernment begins early. Giving students a breadth of good books helps them develop a taste for beautiful illustrations, elevated, articulate language, and virtuous action. When we provide good choices early, students are better able to make good choices independently later.
4. **CONFIDENCE**: Reading 100 books in 100 days is no small feat for a new reader! Nothing breeds success like success itself. Achieving this goal gives students confidence in their ability and courage to tackle future difficult challenges. Students, furthermore, begin to recognize that accomplishment itself is its own reward!

HOW TO USE THIS BOOK

The **100 Books in 100 Days Challenge** asks all rising first grade students to read 100 books—ideally one book per day during the summer.

- One page is allotted for each book completed. Students should write the title of the book completed on the lines provided. If space and time allow, the name of the author and a short comment or description could be added. Parents may want to model text for neatness. Space is also provided to draw a picture.
- Students are encouraged to read high-quality literature at their reading ability. We have provided some suggestions in the Appendix; however, students are not limited to this list. Books of varying degrees of difficulty are provided. Use this list as a starting point—but keep in mind it is by no means exhaustive.
- Parents are also encouraged to use the read-aloud book lists scheduled in the Core Curriculum packages and found at MemoriaPress.com/curriculum/read-aloud-packages. Having heard these stories already, students may feel more confident in attempting to read them independently. Keep in mind, read-aloud selections are often slightly above independent reading ability. Consider using the lists at or below grade level.
- While not required, we do recommend that parents listen as students read aloud and supervise reading for completion and comprehension. Students at this stage often need assistance and encouragement. Remind students to mind punctuation. Encourage persistence in sounding out phonetic words. When advanced words appear, offer help and definitions.
- Have fun! While this may seem a daunting task, it affords a great opportunity for quality reading time together and promotes the development of habits that will serve your young student for a lifetime!

STUDENT GUIDELINES

1. Students should hold pencils properly.

Left-handed Right-handed

2. Start each line close to the left margin and don't cross the right margin.
3. Uppercase letters must touch the top and bottom lines.
4. Most lowercase letters start at the middle, dashed line.
5. Lowercase b, d, f, h, k, and l are all tall letters that touch the top line.
6. Lowercase g, j, p, q, and y have hooks or tails that cross the bottom line.
7. All words should be one pinky space apart.
8. Letters should all stand tall and straight.
9. Erase mistakes completely and be neat.

I

4

6

8

10

13

17

20

22

25

29

40

47

50

88

90

100

APPENDIX

SUPPLEMENTAL READING LIST

Below are the suggested additional literature selections for the challenge beyond the classroom read alouds. Titles are arranged by author and are graduated by degree of difficulty. The easier titles by the author will be listed first.

P.D. Eastman Beginning Books
Go, Dog. Go!
I'll Teach My Dog 100 Words
Snow
Are You My Mother?
Big Dog…Little Dog
The Best Nest
A Fish Out of Water

Simms Taback
Joseph Had a Little Overcoat

Peter Eastman
Fred and Ted Like to Fly
Fred and Ted Go Camping
Fred and Ted's Road Trip

B. Wiseman
Morris the Moose
Morris the Moose Goes to School

Alice Schertle
Little Blue Truck
Little Blue Truck Leads the Way

Mem Fox
Time For Bed

Michael Rosen
We're Going on a Bear Hunt

Dr. Seuss's Beginning Book Collection
Ten Apples up on Top!
Green Eggs and Ham
Hand, Hand, Fingers, Thumb
Hop on Pop
Put Me in the Zoo
One Fish, Two Fish, Red Fish, Blue Fish
The Cat in the Hat
Mr. Brown Can Moo! Can You?
Dr. Seuss's ABC
Fox in Socks

Alyssa Satin Capucilli
Bathtime for Biscuit
Meet Biscuit!
Biscuit's New Trick

Reeve Lindbergh
The Day the Goose Got Loose

Peggy Parrish
Play Ball, Amelia Bedelia
Amelia Bedelia
Amelia Bedelia and the Surprise Shower
(Each chapter can count as one book.)

Syd Hoff
Sammy the Seal
Danny and the Dinosaur
Mrs. Brice's Mice

Arnold Lobel
Mouse Soup
Frog and Toad All Year
Days with Frog and Toad
Frog and Toad Together
Owl at Home
Frog and Toad Are Friends
(Each chapter can count as one book.)

Eileen Spinelli
Silly Tilly's Valentine
Silly Tilly's Thanksgiving Dinner
Silly Tilly and the Easter Bunny
Silly Tilly

Wanda Gag
The ABC Bunny

Else Minarik
A Kiss for Little Bear
Little Bear's Visit
Little Bear
(Each chapter can count as one book.)

Leonard Kessler
Stan the Hot Dog Man
Mr. Pine's Purple House
Mr. Pine's Mixed-up Signs

H.A. Rey
Curious George Goes Camping
Curious George Flies a Kite
Curious George and the Puppies

Eric Carle
Brown Bear, Brown Bear, What Do You See?
The Very Busy Spider
The Very Hungry Caterpillar
The Tiny Seed
Little Cloud
The Mixed-up Chameleon
Polar Bear, Polar Bear, What Do You Hear?
The Foolish Tortoise

Karma Wilson
Bear Says Thanks
Bear Snores On

Miryam
The Happy Man and His Dump Truck

Joan L. Nodset
Go Away, Dog

Richard Scarry
Busiest Fire Fighters Ever
Please and Thank You Book

Cynthia Rylant
Mr. Putter & Tabby Feed the Fish
Mr. Putter & Tabby Ring the Bell
Mr. Putter & Tabby Clear the Decks
Henry & Mudge and the Long Weekend
Henry & Mudge and the Forever Sea
Henry & Mudge the First Book
(Each chapter can count as one book.)

Easy Reader Classics by Sterling House
The Wind in the Willows
Tom Sawyer
The Jungle Book
Treasure Island
Dr. Dolittle
(Each chapter can count as one book.)

Kevin Henkes
Kitten's First Full Moon
Jessica
Owen

Audrey Penn
The Kissing Hand

Ester Averill
The Fire Cat

Barbara Emberley
Drummer Hoff

Bill Martin, Jr.
Chicka Chicka 1 2 3
Chicka Chicka Boom Boom

Eloise Wilkin
Eloise Wilkin Stories (Little Golden Book Treasury)

Golden Children's Books
The Little Red Caboose
The House that Jack Built
Baby Farm Animals
The Happy Man and His Dump Truck
The Little Red Hen
Noah's Ark
Bible Stories of Boys and Girls
The Poky Little Puppy
Baby Animals

Margaret Wise Brown
Little Fur Family
Big Red Barn
Home for a Bunny
The Color Kittens
The Golden Egg Book
The Runaway Bunny
Bunny's Noisy Book

Crockett Johnson
Harold and the Purple Crayon

Ruth Krauss
The Carrot Seed

Mary Ann Hoberman
It's Simple, Said Simon
Whose Garden Is It?
The Seven Silly Eaters

Tomie DePaolo
Little Mother Goose
The Quilt Story
Charlie Needs a Cloak

Janet Ahlberg
Each Peach Pear Plum

Emmy Payne
Katy No-Pocket

Audrey Wood
The Napping House

Laura Numeroff
If You Give a Mouse a Cookie
If You Take a Mouse to School

Ezra Jack Keats
The Snowy Day

Watty Piper
The Little Engine That Could

Lillian Hoban
Arthur's Honey Bear
Bread and Jam for Frances
A Birthday for Frances
Best Friends for Frances

Jan Karon
Miss Fannie's Hat

Jack Kent
The Caterpillar and the Polliwog

Don Freeman
Corduroy
A Pocket for Corduroy
Norman the Doorman

Seymour Fleishman
The Little Old Man Who Could Not Read

National Geographic –I Can Read Books
(Be sure to pre-read titles not listed.)
From Seed to Plant
Owls
Turtles
Ponies
Manatees
Planets
Elephants

Gene Zion
No Roses for Harry!
Harry and the Lady Next Door
Harry the Dirty Dog

Jan Brett
The Mitten
The Hat
The Three Snow Bears

C.W. Anderson
Billy and Blaze and the Forest Fire
Blaze Shows the Way
Blaze and the Spotted Pony
Blaze and Thunderbolt
Billy and Blaze
(Each chapter can count as one book.)

Poetry
Prayers for Children by Eloise Wilkin
A Child's Book of Poems by Gyo Fujikawa
Llama Who Had No Pajama by Mary Ann Hoberman
My First Real Mother Goose
A Child's Garden of Verses by Robert Louis Stevenson
Animals, Animals by Eric Carle